BOUQUET
OF
STARS

POETRY CHAPEL VOL. III

BOUQUET OF STARS

Chelan Harkin
and Friends

POETRY CHAPEL
PRESS

Author website: www.chelanharkin.com
Editors website: www.davidtensen.com
Editors email: david@davidtensen.com

Poetry Chapel ® Press
Brisbane, QLD, Australia

Cover Illustration: by Jordan Elaine Boyce

Edited: David Tensen & Rachel Huckel

Also available in eBook.

Bouquet of Stars / Chelan Harkin and Friends.
ISBN 978-0-6456072-0-8

Dedicated to
the radical lovers
of all the things
the cosmos
cradles them
with.

Table of Contents

Poetry Chapel Poets

Tracy Brown

Beverly M Frederick

Kristen Guerrero

Susie Rafferty Glad

Velusia Van Horssen

Elaine M Watson

Chelan Harkin

Chelan Harkin has always had a close connection with the spiritual world. She is a loving, ecstatic and expressive spirit with an intimacy in her soul that she longs to share with the whole world. Poetry is one of her favorite, most satisfying ways to accomplish this.

Chelan comes with years of writing experience and two beautiful self-published collections to her name. Her work is highly influenced by other mystical poets including Hafiz and Rumi and has reached an international audience. Chelan's poetry has been highly regarded by American poetry and interpreter of mystical poetry Daniel Ladinsky.

Also by Chelan Harkin:

Susceptible to Light
Poetry by Chelan Harkin. -2020

Let Us Dance!
The Stumble And Whirl With The Beloved. 2021

Support Chelan by purchasing via
www.ChelanHarkin.com

e: chelanharkin@gmail.com
ig: @chelanharkin

fb: /Chelan Harkin Poetry

FOREWORD

Poetry is an invitation for soul liberation. It offers a platform for otherwise disallowed truths to be spoken. I see poetry as perhaps the most effective and radical medium to speak the world we hope to create into being. It communicates its truths in a way that can disarm people and truly impact them rather than create more opinionated walls. I feel poetry to be the most profound gift of my life. It has courted such a deep relationship with my soul.

I grew up both loving the teachings of my family's religion, The Baha'i Faith, but also feeling ill-equipped to translate those teachings into a relationship with God, my deep self, and the world in a way that felt truly satisfying.

Born a deeply sensitive and perceptive truth-teller, I lacked mentorship in how to navigate these giftings. I struggled mightily with a sense of belonging, assuming my feelings and insights were liabilities to connection rather than potential assets. Because I didn't have the skills, support or maturity to navigate my inner world, I decided it safest to stuff it all down and avoid the inner wild-lands of self and God.

Mercifully, this repressing of all that mattered caused me unbearable suffering that drove me to explore a new way. And when my paradigm of repression entered a process of profound undoing at age 21, something of my soul emerged to experiment more with expressing itself to the world and it found a deep and welcoming home in poetry.

While creating poetry has been the most meaningful and satisfying time of my life, it's also been one of deep solitude and aloneness. So when I was offered the opportunity to host this Poetry Chapel space, it was an interesting adjustment to imagine including a community into this very personal poetic space of mine. At the same time, I found this Poetry Chapel model, so beautifully envisioned and created by David Tensen, to be irresistibly wonderful.

Remembering myself in my pre-publication days without a clue about how to put my poetry into book form and share it with the world, I truly couldn't have imagined anything better than an explicitly emotionally and relationally safe space characterized by encouragement that would include step by step publishing guidance, a network, insights into the marketing process and ultimately a book that included my work! It was impossible to say no to offering something like this and this experience has been a true gift in my life.

Poetry Chapel has been so deeply nourishing - not simply because of the group's inspired words but because of their open-hearted bravery week after week in sharing their poems within the profound experience of sacred trust that sharing poetry creates. To be able to have the honor of glimpsing another's soul as they recite their poetry is perhaps an unmatchable honor. It is with great joy and profound pride that I find my name beside the others in this book. I applaud the effort and beauty, consideration, bravery and time everyone poured into this project. And I have been indelibly impacted and moved by their words.

I dedicate my part of this book to each of them with the deepest bow.

With gratitude and love,

Chelan

While I Walk This Earth

My dear Creator,
while I walk this earth

help me unlock
dancing from the feet,
truth from the tongue,
rejoicing from the spirit,
springtime from the heart.

Make my pen a key
that I may unlock poetry
from the world.

I Can't Say Why

I can't say why
the moon decided
to whisper her intimacies
to me

Or why God,
in Her nightly romantic whimsy,
let me in on Her pillow talk.

I don't know how
I learned to read
the calligraphy of silver rivers

Or why the stars
included me among their scribes
and passed me some of their light ink
to bring their distant glow
closer.

It is an embarrassment of riches
that Autumn has allowed me
to translate her,

That the burgeoning desires
of spring
have made my heart a confidant,

And that the forest has opened
the secrets of her body
to receive me

It's an unspeakable honor
that so much truth
in humanity's undercurrents
has swept my pen in
to write of this wild flow.

I'm not sure why
I was asked to join
The Church of All Things

But I am so, so grateful
to have been shown
that each atom is a holy place

and no matter what we do
our life is an animated prayer
becoming increasingly self-aware
about the ecstasy
of its devotion.

Hollow Bone

My temple
most often
has been the hollow bone
of loneliness

my spirituality,
discovering music
that sings there.

My growth,
almost entirely,
has come
from the desperate wailing
of the seed of my heart

needing to crack open holes
for breathing
in the dark room
of its hopelessness

to deprive itself less
of taking new light
all the way in.

I become sanctified
when my frailties bleed out
and there's no balm to grab
save the salve
of Her verse

that doesn't so much close the wound
as give purpose
to its pouring.

My life's fruits have bloomed
from being such a barren snag
that I had to graft parts of myself
to God.

We must be careful
lest we elevate people
for anything holy they produce.

More often than not
anything that can truly reach a heart

comes from a heart
whose wounds
have become so unbearable
they must burst
into song.

Crushed Into Wine

As a grape
ripens
until it is ready
to be crushed
into wine

so too does your pain
ripen within you
until it is ready
to be crushed
into love.

It's when, in the blindness
of our anguish,
we forget
the destiny of all hearts
is Love's great barrel
that suffering
takes such hold.

The missing ingredient
for peace
as you ripen
toward Love's obliteration
of complete becoming
is trust
in The Vintner's
sacred timing.

The brand of your love
is a particular variety
and She cherishes
all those nuanced notes
you've gathered
into yourself
and called suffering
that now make you so
exceptionally fine
and sweet..

Every Luminous Thing

May you remember
you and every luminous thing
share an origin story.

The Seed of My Heart

I feel God
germinating the seed
of my heart
again

new life bursting
out through me

breaking down
all that I've known

that She may have more space
to love the world
through me.

Bed Chambers

An ecstatic poem
is the climax

from the conjugal visit
between the wildly divine
and achingly human

in the bed chambers
of the heart.

The Holy One

Let baptism not be
an exclusively religious thing

May each of us have a ceremony
as often as the reminder is needed

for community to gather around us
to witness

a grandmother
or a child
or simply the clouds
that water spring

anoint our brows,
sprinkle our heads
with water's kiss of devotion
and whisper in our ear,

"We acknowledge the holy one
you've always been."

A Conservative Estimate

They say there's a 1 in 30 trillion chance
of you existing at all...

but I think that's a conservative estimate.

When you factor in
that a universe happened
to explode from something
the size of a marble, or a pin prick,
we immediately move beyond incalculability.

And adding the unlikelihood
that the destruction of that blast
would have created
a vast city of stars
with a place tucked into it
called earth

that would be soft and fertile enough
to accommodate the holy and mysterious concept of
"mother",

the odds become wilder yet.

And then that the waves
of this mighty thing
we've come to call the sea

had some great tidal moment
that washed your sea-born, squid-like
prehistoric ancestors
into each others arms or tentacles or fins
to procreate the possibility of you.

Or consider all the phenomena that led
a later ancestor out of his cave
to follow a trail of pheromones
toward your hairy
very great, great grandmother
to grunt at her in some alluring way.

Or simply that your mother
held a magical jewel inside of her
that carried half of the potential
of your DNA,
which is just scientific jargon for,
"The scripture of You"

and that a magnetic force called love is here
that pulled your father toward her.

What is the equation
for water existing
to quench your longing for it?

Or that an asteroid crashed
into the dinosaurs
at just the right moment
to give mammals the possibility of ascendance?

Or that each ice age froze
and thawed time
just so
to create the propitious conditions
for life's waters
to flow in your direction?

How might we sum up the truth
that you would not be here
were it not for every other luminous
pulse and beat and song and swell
of this magnificent, wonder drenched
system of stars and death and wombs
and the great explosion of life?

What exponents would suffice
to express that every minute and magnificent
happening
throughout the eternity of beginning-less time
has necessitated your life?

There is no number we could give
that could equal the astronomical mystery
of life's grand total
of you.

You are unbelievable—
as unlikely as God.

Dear one, we just have to round it all up
to miracle.

No Other Side

The ancestors are here with us
right now.

Not only are we not alone

we are surrounded by the vast community
of our blood line,
it flows through us—
through tributary veins
into river arteries
into the great sea
of the collective heart.

Some ancestors are holding our hand

Some are pouring poetry through us

Some are still trying to work their stuff out through
our bones

Some are what make us sing

We are not ourselves, in the isolated way we've
come to think of it

We are a quilt of our lineage

We are an intimate ecosystem
of our grandparents roots

We are connected not only
to all that is currently living now

but to all from the past
and all who will come

There is no other side of the veil—
we are already there.

Our perception simply hasn't opened yet.

The World Needs Your Voice

The world needs your voice.

Not your voice trying
to look like my voice

Or his or her voice.

Even trying to craft your voice
to look like the greats—Rumi
or Hafiz, Dickinson or Yeats

will be a fruitless ploy.

It is not the voice that comes
from trying to please Jesus or God
or that anyone on Facebook
will approve of
that is called for.

The world wants your voice
that bubbles up from the depths,

The voice that comes from listening
to whatever is alive in your deep heart.

Dig deep into your latent magma
and erupt your sorrow onto the page.

Step out of the robe of your facade
and show your truth to us trembling.

Whatever your writer's block
dip your pen into the heart of its reasons
and tell about that,

about the flat lands
with no topography of inspiration
you've been wandering down
for so long,

about how muse seems
an endangered species—

let us feel your drought of God.

Tell us about the curvature
of the ice block of your numbness
and all the factors
that have carved its shape.

Tell us of your affairs
with loneliness
and how you can't seem to stop returning
to her cold bed.

Talk about the writers you're jealous of -
how all you want to do is sign your name
to their flame.

Invite us into the catacombs of your fears.

Show us the graveyards in your heart
filled with all the beloved things
you've lost.

Don't just give us pictures
of the bathed, swaddled baby—
the tidy aftermath—

we want to know the pangs
of how you've birthed yourself
or aborted this process
time and time again.

Yearning is the siren
that summons the writer—
sing us her song.

Writing has nothing to do
with crafting perfect, calligraphied words—
grab the inkwell and spill your truth.

Let your words reek of sweat and light
and carry hints
of the toil and deep breath
of your ancestors
and the notes of any song
they stored away to pass down to you.

A poem is where the flint of soul
strikes the stone of trauma

and makes a spark.

A poem is a thumbprint of the soul
and the page wants you
to leave your evidence.

The world needs your voice.

Un-sheath your knowing.

You have permission
to say anything.

The Winter Snag

The winter snag was sure
God had forsaken her.

She used to be all flourishing,
vibrant and full of fruit and offerings!

Creatures were attracted to her!
Butterflies, birds and bees
were her devotees
coming daily to kiss
the heart of her flowers.

People came to pluck and celebrate
her fruits.

And now look at her!
Hard, cold, lifeless limbs—
her branches like gnarled hands
in the frozen posture
of an arthritic prayer.

But dear one, God is not just
an active, blossoming force.

She lives in the quietudes of winter.

She is the gathering of potential
in your long, silent seasons.

She is not just found in the quenching—
She is your soul's thirst.

She is the decomposition
that the new may have its blossom.

She is the silence
that has composed the music.

„Give me a sign!"
We pound our chests and demand
at the sky

While God is the huddled energy
inside your indirection.

"Give me an answer!"
We holler

When God is also the question.

"Show me the way!"
We shout at God,
The Great Wanderer.

She has not abandoned you
when She's tending to your journey
inside the exquisite mystery
of Her secret silence.

We Drink the Same Water

We drink the same water
that dinosaurs drank,

that Muhammad used
for his ablutions,

that Jesus used
to wash his disciples' feet,

that our ancestors emerged from
to try legs,

the same water that crashes
in a quintessence
of creation's power
at the base
of Niagara Falls,

that so beautifully helped your mother
hold you
as your light grew within her
its lamp
of a body.

We drink the same water
that has lived inside each other's tears—

some deep part of us
has tasted the suffering of all

and the tenderness.

Most of our bodies are made of tributaries, rivers,
oceans and clouds

we all cycle through each other,

we are Everest's mists,

we are the evaporation
from The Amazon,

we are the atmosphere.

We drink the same water
that is imprinted with the ecstasy
of the estuary
as the river embraces the sea,

of the unconditional baptism of rain—
the heavens have always known
the whole earth is holy,

of the rainforest
absorbing the full roar
of the downpour of the sky
back into its wild being,

of each dew drop
that proposes to morning
with its field of glistening diamonds,

of every tincture and tonic
and stew and broth
that has been brewed to heal.

We are made of ancient water
and our makeup is continually recycled
through the heavens.

Fully Human

Comedians need a space to cry

And spiritual leaders need a space
to share their insecurities
and how vulnerable they feel.

Religious people need a space
to share their doubts

And priests need a space to confess
their desires

Mothers need a space to wail
about how regularly
we long to escape motherhood

And parents need permission
to curl their hurts into fetal position
and cradle their hearts.

It must be okay for saints
to also have scuff marks

And for the monk to long
to come down from the mountaintop.

Doctors need a space
to talk about their addictions,

Mystics must be allowed
to also trudge
through the mundane,

And we need to be able to tell God
we hate Him
now and then
to stay in honest and whole relationship.

Dear one, to be fully human,
we must be allowed to share
our full experience
of strength and struggle
in a way that doesn't threaten our belonging

We must grow into hearts
that can hold all parts of each other.

For our light
to go on sustaining itself
it must be allowed its shadow.

The Full Moon

"I've arrived!"
said the full moon.

"I've figured it out!
I'll stay whole this time,
I won't wane anymore,
no more darkness!"

And hasn't your heart
thought the same thing
right before another plunge
into its necessary school
of shadows?

To insist on staying light
is unnatural
and without elegance.

Darling, learn the rhythms
of descent
into your precious darkness.

The moon would be much less alluring,
would have no message to teach
and her process
would be much less poetic
if she only knew the luminous side
of her wholeness.

Hear the Universe

"Why is it that so often
the sensitive ones
are the poets?"

"Because, my dear,
they need to be tuned in enough
to hear The Universe.

Real and True and Alive

One day, and really before long,
my body will pass
and everything I've clung to
and every way I've gained a name
in this world
will be laid to rest.

My hands will have become snags,
no longer fruit bearing
and life will have written her last signatures
into the lines on my face.

Gravity will have had its way
with my saggy breasts
and my body of work
will be devoured by the worms of time

And everything that was ever real
and true and alive in me
will still be real and true
and alive in me then.

And one day, and really
not long after that,
every cherished accomplishment
this world has ever produced
and every mind
who might remember them
and every exquisite thing
that has ever been
will be ground to dust

34

and the sun will eat the earth
and a black hole will engulf the sun

and all that is real and true
and alive in me now
will be real and true and alive
in me then.

Ancestral Line

This one is for any woman
in my ancestral line
who swung her hips
while hanging the wash.

This one is for any woman
in my line
who mixed sunshine
into the bread dough
for breakfast
that she would be a participant
in helping morning rise.

This one is for any woman
for whom the primordial form
of the holy word, "No"
began forming in her gut,
in her root,
in the deepest furrows
of her knowing

and for she
who tended the spark
of the first flame
of justice
coming from tasting her worth
that still went unconsidered
until it began
to flicker and grow
and imagine itself
in the torch
it would one day
hand to me.

This is for the women
who died clutching buried dreams
to their chests
that those jewels
would be passed down
for that propitious time
in which the world would be
powerful and tender enough
to be ready to receive the howling
of their most wild prayers.

This is for the fire
in the women that was never fed
that we may rise Phoenix-like
from their ashes
to spread our wingspan farther
to honor all the ways they were not
allowed to fully fly.

With Love

With love
eternity is infused
into every otherwise
mortal moment.

The Sacred Exchange

The sacred exchange:
Your pain hands you wisdom
when you give it love.

This Idea of Finding Yourself

Don't get too hung up
on this idea of finding yourself,
some of us are essence in motion—
a dance,
not a freeze frame.

Let the particle
of your identity crash
into a wave of light.

God will catch it
and ride you
to a new shore
of unforeseen discoveries.

Darling, what's to find?

There is nothing solvable
about the soul.

Self-discovery is simply
to become more
and more in awe

of our unfoldment
into a wellspring
of enlivened mystery.

Approach Thirsty

Lately I've been praying to Muhammad,
Moses, Krishna, Buddha, Baha'u'llah, Zoroaster,
Jesus—
why be choosy?

I ask any source of true love
and great joy
to throw me as many bones
as they might.

Sometimes I prayer to Mozart, Bach or Galileo
to pour music or the stars
through me.

Often I pray to Tahirih,
a great Persian poet and feminist
of the 1800's who would remove
her veil when addressing men
and was martyred
for speaking the irrepressible truth
in her heart
at age 38.

Her final words were,
"You can kill me as soon as you like,
but you will never stop
the emancipation of women."

I often ask Hafiz for a dance
and we go for the most poetic whirls.

Sometimes I ask Rumi
that he pluck me an ancient,
everblooming rose
and I crush its scent
onto the page.

I have a crush on Khalil Gibran
and ask that he pass me
inspired love notes.

I pray to Harriet Tubman,
that queen of heroism,
for courage
and to Einstein
for out of this world ideas.

Inspiration is not elitist.
There is no muse
that is off limits,
no genius you should not approach
and ask to be yours.

There are no copyright issues
with what you receive from prayer.

No one lays claim
to certain frequencies
of light.

Oh, beseech whoever you might
that the master keys
that open all hearts
are put in your care
that your particularly necessary
style of expression
may open new portals of beauty
to the eyes of the world.

Hobnob with all the great
dead poets,
thinkers,
lovers,
artists,
heroes of justice,
leaders of truth.
They still want a place
to pour their wonder
into the world
and you are a worthy vessel.

It's an open bar in the sky.
Approach thirsty,
and ask!

A Temple

Your body is a temple
where your consciousness goes
to pray.

Make Little Joy Spots

Make little joy spots
in the Universe

with the way you speak,
love, beautify a space,
care for each other,
dance.

Build small temples
of each moment.

Unhitch your happiness
from every justification
and watch God
ripple out from you.

You are a sanctuary in motion
that can creatively pour
light from yourself.

Touch the earth
in a way that makes her smile—
you are the world's
beauty mark.

Say yes to that
which creates little joy spots
in the Universe.

Tender Cradle

You see how the light
of the crescent moon
is such a tender cradle
for her darkness.

Oh, you too
can grow into
holding your shadows
like that.

Approach Gently

At least daily,
approach gently

the quivering bird
of your heart

and whisper,
„I'll never leave you."

The Moon Let Go Of Everything

And the stars bade me,

"Unhitch yourself
from the world
and come toward us.

The moon let go of everything
and her light
never trembles."

A Total Breakdown

"She's having a total breakdown,"

One put together
and very self-satisfied seed
with no cracks in it
whispered to another
about a third seed who had begun
to germinate.

"She's completely falling apart—
her life is a mess!"

They gazed superiorly
at the smooth, intact facade
of their shells
that so perfectly upheld
the expectations of the status quo.

Clearly, compared to that wild,
sprouting seed
disrupting the peace,
they were doing something right...right?

But now and then,
they secretly looked up
with longing
at the tall stemmed
beautiful and bravely opened flower nearby
wondering if there might be more
to themselves.

And one day,
when the inward agony
of maintaining the appearance
of an outwardly perfect
and tidy life
became too much,

the seed scooched herself
close to the flower
and asked in hushed tones,
"How do I become more like you?"

And the flower smiled,
"You must first be willing
to have a total breakdown
of every identity you've known
and then you must be so bold
as to let your previously predictable life
become a wild, sacred mess."

God Did It

The light of God
Is the only revolutionary.

It's what we look away from
In each other's eyes,

It's the light
that's too bright
to see
even within our own selves.

It's the dethroning bliss
that overthrows
the old comforts
of every convincing sadness
we've clung to.

It dismantles
individuality
and tosses your identity
into the sea that cannot be separated
from all.

As Her revolution builds
in our hearts
humanity evolves.

She is the Great Subversive One
who will speak up
for that which is true
even amidst those armed
with the harshest dedication
to falsehoods
because She is that
which cannot die.

She was the lead abolitionist.
She was at the front
of the feminist marches,
She is the origin
of any cause
that brings consciousness
forward.

If any religious dogmatists
or puffed up men
get mad at me
for the great mercy
of my disruptive poetry
that calls out all
that isn't your worthiness,

She has told me
to use Her
as my scapegoat.

So I look at them
unflinchingly
with a wry smile
and say,

"Don't blame me.
God did it."

No Therapy Compares

There is no therapy
that quite compares
with immersing yourself
in nature

To witness the nightly bloom
of the rose gold moon,

To let the friction
of the crickets' song
re-spark something in your heart,

To sleep under the stars,
that blueprint of understanding
into how little we know
of the luminous reality
of God

and let something of the universe
begin to hum in you again.

Curiosity
is generous enough
to find us out here
as we begin again
to become enlivened
with the unanswerable.

Be near
unto a clear mountain stream
and a sacred element in the heart
becomes clarified.

The outdoors isn't native land
for man-made pressures
and fastidiousness.

Worries don't know
how to sustain themselves
in this territory
and slowly fall away.

"How easy can it be
to remake ourselves?"
I ask myself
as I recline into the woods
and intentionally do nothing
but ask the intelligent hands
of Life
to unspin me of all
that isn't Her oneness.

The forest is represented
by the greatest diplomat,
Holy Silence,
who shows us something
of our mortality
and that there's nothing
to fear of it.

Something of The Mountains

When I die, dear God,
please, let me take something
of the mountains with me.

May I stow away,
inside some caverns of myself,
a glow from the moon?

Let me fill
any pockets my soul might have
with bits of silver rivers
and quiet moments
of starlight.

Can I pack a bag before I go
and bring only sunrise?

May I keep a souvenir
from whatever it is
Autumn does to the heart?

Mustn't it be continuous,
this sacred inadequacy
of bearing the beautiful burden
of love
that at once sears and sings
and is the reason why
I grow?

Tell me that is an empire
that cannot fall.

How many songs may I take?

Please say you have room
for all my laughter
and the vast collection of diamonds
that are my tears?

May I be rich enough
to bring remembrance
of the way
the jewelled stars
coronate the night?

Can I bring a moment
of that eternal peace
found in the spirit
of the forest's exhale
after the rain?

Please, may our passage
into the Beyond
only widen our access
to the spectrum of beauty.

Though my wildest imagination
cannot possibly believe anything
could be better
than a naked sole
pressed into the dew-drenched grass
of this utterly love-soaked earth

or to be woken early enough
to be kissed alive
by the dawn.

Please, still, may the Beyond
be a space
where I may feel
a closer kinship
with the heart of everything
I've come to love
here.

Great Mirage

That your heart
is a small, beating, mortal thing
is really a great mirage,

an incredible sleight of hand!

Inside you'll find
an unfolding landscape
of God—

The mystery within moons,
the grandeur within mountains
and a limitless, limitless
Love

that could never be bound
by anything so small
as death.

A New World

Let the sword
that pierces your pride
cut so deeply

And trace its blade
in and down
to the most humble wound
that has too long been defended
by your reactions.

Stay there
as you weep out the poison
of hiding

and enter the wellspring
you once thought a wound
that gushes self understanding
and forgiveness.

Stay there and experience
transformation
as your deepest shames
given to light
become your flags of honor

in the great victory
of no longer having
to reject yourself.

It is in that heroic lack
of hiding your hurt

that you let God's grace
into your heart

You are changing the world
through changing your patterns,
by feeling your pain
all the way through
to the point where it blooms
forgiveness.

You are remaking the past now
with your courage
to no longer store pain
that inevitably ferments
into an arsenal.

You are melting those guns
into shovels
and with them
you are turning the soil
that will grow a new world.

The Bursting Allium

The bursting allium
tells you everything you need to know
about God,

The wild strawberry
so saturated with flavor,

The impossibly intricate
and delicate fabric
of any petal,

Even the beauty
in the breakdown
of the rusted garden gate—
if it catches your noticing just right
it too creaks of the sacred.

Have you ever let yourself
be photosynthesized
by the blossoming
peach tree—
let it take you
all the way in
to its sweetness?

Or read the palm
of a leaf—
every unique etching
another way to say
"Beauty was here."

Make it Their Medium

Rumi's heart,
more than an orb
of unattainable light
set above you,

was more likely
a hopelessly unfixable
broken pot

through which light
was merciful enough
to continually spill.

Hafiz, most likely,
was a gardener
of sorrow—
he knew how to bring its aching
to blossom
and open you to beauty there.

I'm sorry if this disappoints you
that even the greats
aren't elitist untouchables
that have defied suffering.

Even Jesus, Muhammad, The Buddha—
all those Great Ones
must have held tenderly
in their own chests
the deepest ravines of humanity's sorrow—
how else could they have known
compassion like that?

They simply knew
how to kneel down deep enough
to kiss that wound.

Don't do that unnatural thing
of separating the sacred
from its sorrow

Artists of the deep heart
are not apart from suffering
they've learned the craft
of melting it into gold.

They don't flee from fire
they make it their medium.

Tiny Sprout

What would happen
if we could be as satisfied
by the tiny sprout
emerging from the ground
as we are about a big promotion?

As infatuated
with the newly opened daffodil
as we might be with a new lover?

What if we noticed
the detail of a leaf
or the mood of the forest
after a rain
at least as closely as we notice
our own shortcomings?

How do we re-sensitize our hearts
to feel the staggering love
poured upon the world
from the blush of each sunset?

How do we prioritize
our gratitude
so that instead of consuming
the whole earth
in a way that will never fill us
a single dew drop
could satisfy our thirsts?

Every part of us is an antenna for beauty,
a receptor for divine tenderness—
what if we didn't need so much stimulus
to connect with that and live again?

What might it be like
if we could take the hierarchy
out of experience,
judging some moments as worthy
and insensitively tromping over others?

And instead, began to walk slowly
and with bare feet
over every precious moment
of our lives
kissing the earth
with our soles

in the practice of being
so replete
with sacred wonder

and quenched with the recognition
that nothing about ourselves
or this life
requires even a drop
of enhancement.

Awakening Is Messy

Awakening is messy.

You don't transcend
into some paradisiacal,
elitist inner garden.

It doesn't perfect you.

You first come into
all the reasons you've so wanted
to stay asleep—

and there are many
very good reasons.

We awaken to all the reasons
we've so wanted
to disassociate from our bodies,
those storehouses of pain and God—
to enter through either of these doors
is to have stripped from you
the illusion of smallness.

Sleeping was relatively painless,
in its numbed way.

To awaken, really,
is to begin to feel.

As we feel through more pain
we feel more compassion.

Awakening is bit by bit
coming out of denial
around all the reasons you've needed
to wield
that terrible tool of "othering"—

because so much
was unbearable
inside of our own self.

Awakening is diving
into the cracks in our hearts
rather than mortaring them.

It does not look like being
perfectly empowered,
seamlessly composed—
It's to commit with all your heart
to no longer take out your helplessness
on anyone else.

Awakening has nothing to do
with stern, stoic spirituality.

It has nothing to do
with finally being aloof enough
to not be impacted by the gifts
of your beautiful feelings.

Awakening isn't only for special people.
We're all on our way
toward coming out of the sleep cycle.

Awakening is the at times compass-less
and often inglorious
inner odyssey
toward the rough ruby of all that is bruised
and true in our hearts

It is bushwhacking
through a tangled history
of acquired conditioning
of all that we are not.

Awakening is messy—
Be not fooled.

The myth that awakening
looks anything like spiritual perfectionism
is perhaps the best sleeping pill.

Wild Grace

Put me amidst life's
simplest things

that give their lives to blooming
or quietly glowing
without reaching for a name.

Position my gratitude suchly
that my heart gets all it needs
met from sunlight

And open me in a way
that allows silence
to be a deep source of nourishment.

Let me gather the great bundle
of my every mistake and shortcoming
into my arms like a vast bouquet
and thank it for making
a gentler and more honest place
out of my heart.

God, remind me of the great laughter
that I am
and let this remembrance dissolve away
illusion like steam

May I settle into belonging
here in the humble majesty
of the verdant, breathing cathedral
of this forest

and may you hear my prayer:

I want no spiritual mastery
but to be porous
like the earth
to the nourishing rain

and to receive whatever amount
of the great blessing of grace
my small heart is able to bear.

May I never again
attempt the arrogance
of trying to conquer
another's heart—
let me be a great ally
to its freedom.

May I settle in
to feeling everything

so that no love that masks
as grief or fear or despair
may escape me.

Dear God, if you please,
no more of this distance.
Plant yourself in my body.
I want nothing
but to be alive
with Wild Grace.

It's Not So Much That I Want to Know God

It's not so much that I want
to know God

As to be close to the spiral
in the seashell,

To feel the wind
as my own breath,

To let birdsong all the way in
to my being,
let my bones
be the ledger lines
for its dancing song.

It's not so much
that I want to know God

as to be reacquainted
with the intimacies of the stars
through remembering
they've always shone from within
the expansiveness of my own chest

It's not so much that I want
to please any Cosmic Authority
as to be strong enough
to finally hold every little girl still inside of me
as she weeps old tears
that were never held.

It's not so much that I need a particular
place of worship—

I want to flee less
the majesty of each moment
that the humble door
of my ancient heart
might be more willing to open
to the wide beauty
of the world.

My only prayer is to be excommunicated
from ideology

and join the congregation of morning dew
shimmering with enlivened mystery
and freshness,
replete with sparkling wonder.

It's not so much
that I want to worship God

as for my devotional practice
to be opening
my body to the living scripture
of Life's movement
as She dances Her desires
through me
and to remember
to say thank you
with deep recognition
for every small act of love
that finds me.

It's not so much that I believe in God
as it has been taught

but that all I desire
is to serve
the One Great Heart
that lives within us all.

God Kissed the Devil

When I opened my heart
I caught God
kissing the devil

right there in the bedchambers
of my chest

It was quite the scandal
and pretty much toppled everything.

Right and Wrong were like, "Woah!
We can do that?!"

And rushed into each other's arms.

The affection that began
between Good and Bad
would have been fiercely scorned
by most of the angels
had they been living
by the stringent doctrines of their past

But they'd already stripped naked
and started running
through my whole body
hipping and hollering
and causing a holy raucous
of pure aliveness

In that moment
every evil touched
its original innocence

And nothing could any longer be bothered
with investing its blessed life
in the deadening work of judgement

And as the veil was pulled off
every part of the world
I'd once cloaked in shadow—

suddenly nothing
was not my bride.

SECTION 2

The Poetry Chapel Collective
Volume 3
Chosen Works

Tracy Brown

Guided by Spirit.
Groomed to serve.
Glazed in the fire of business.
Generous with her time and talents.
Grown through prayer.
This is Tracy Brown.

The human experience can be messy and painful. As a poet, I try to capture what it looks, sounds and feels like to apply spiritual values in daily life. I want you to not only recognize Spirit when you are experiencing joy, beauty, love or the magnificence of nature, but to also engage spirituality to navigate the fear, anger and confusion that accompanies real life challenges.

I have applied universal spiritual principles to infuse my life with peace and joy since 1986. As a licensed spiritual coach my focus is to help others integrate their personal, professional and spiritual priorities in ways that ensure they create lives they love.

Please visit me at: www.ReclaimJoy.com. You'll find quotations, prayers, spiritual practices, recorded talks and poetry designed to remind you that "whatever life experience you're in, you can always find joy within."

Toward Good

what if i focused on today
and left yesterday's hurts and heights behind?

what if i accepted the past as complete
and entered every conversation as new?

what if i believed i am One with Spirit
and saw today's experiences as answered prayer?

what if i saw the gift i am receiving
and accepted it without guilt or shame?

i am ready to soar without dragging the weight
of yesterday's choices or challenges.

i am ready to sing without knowing the words
but trusting the melody will suffice.

i am ready to forgive myself and all others,
and look through the lens of Love.

i am ready to trust there is a Power
bigger than me moving my life –

Toward Good.

Control

in a quiet moment
of deep reflection,
she – who created the entire universe –
softly whispered in my ear:

i love you
more than you will ever understand
and will pretty much let you do
whatever you desire.
there is nothing you can imagine that
i am unable to provide.

but please indulge me
and answer this one question:

is it arrogance
or narcissism
that makes you believe
you have the power to be responsible
for the journey
or the choices
of another?

Trust

It is not enough to accept an idea...
It cannot manifest until you trust it as real.
Until you behave as if it is the truth, it cannot live.

It is not enough to tolerate a person
He cannot share with you his unique gifts and talents
Until you trust he is your equal

Until you welcome her
As you would welcome your twin
She cannot reveal her essence.

So do not pretend to love or believe.
Demonstrate your faith by your actions.

Show me what you believe and who you love
By what, and who, you trust.

Sally

you were my first friend and playmate.
neighbors. what fun!
running and playing and giggling
at whatever four-year-old girls giggle about.
we learned that crossing the street
to explore life in another person's yard
is a gateway to new worlds and experiences.

you were my first friend and playmate.
neighbors. what fun!
breaking unknown barriers
building unbreakable bonds
crossing imagined boundaries
cultivating a shared vision
of playing and growing together.

you were my first friend and playmate.
neighbors. what fun!
until that day of reckoning
when four-year-olds learned
there is a hierarchy of humanity
because "people like you"
are not welcome in some homes.

you were my first friend and playmate.
neighbors. what fun!
for four-year-olds to learn their place
adults must tell them lies about race.

Amicably Divorced

it matters little to me what others think about
the books i've written
the places i've been
the people i've met

what i want to be known for is
kindness
compassion
service
growth

i stand for
love in action
bringing people together
growing a bigger pie
(and a better world)

if along the way
i make a name for myself,
that is collateral damage:
important to notice but
nothing to be distracted by

the spotlight has always been on
showing people what god looks like
in human form
and helping them see and be
their own form of divinity

stuff i have done
is not who i am!
i am neither embarrassed
nor impressed
by my achievements

i appreciate my past experiences
as my path of becoming

nothing more
nothing less

think of me as
amicably divorced
from yesterday's joys and pains

i am happily married
to now and tomorrow.

Beverly M Frederick

Beverly M Frederick lives on a small Portuguese island off the coast of Morocco with her partner Douglas Orton. A yogi, poet, songstress and facilitator of ecstatic transformative circles and events she grew up singing in gospel choirs and put herself through school working at dance halls in and around San Francisco.

Before founding The WisdomWay Center in an historical church on Hawaii's Big Island she traveled the world extensively and collaborated for decades with ecofeminist author and activist Starhawk. Other living writers that have had deep and lasting impact are Joanna Macy, Ntozake Shange and Alice Walker.

She has been published in **The Pagan Book of Living and Dying** and **The Twelve Wild Swans**, as well as **The Reclaiming Quarterly, Yoga Journal** and **Spirituality & Health Magazine.**

Many of the chants and songs from her CDs **In the Arms of the Wild, Through the Darkness** and **Sea Sutras** can be found on YouTube.

All can be accessed or purchased at
https://www.beverlyfrederick.org

If something here has touched you she would love to hear your reflections and can be reached at
beverlyfrederick@yahoo.com

For Daryn

I was ready
I thought
prepared
by the numbing
months
watching your
skeleton
emerge

but amongst
our many
friends
at your memorial
I noticed
I had
left
a space
beside
me

Two Hands

waiting for the bus to work
in the predawn dark
two hands
clutch both my shoulders
from behind
"COME WITH ME"
he commands

mine is not a sheltered life
two hands
clutching both shoulders
from behind
is vital information
if both hands hold me
he has
no weapon

FIGHT
my body braces
FIGHT NOW
I crouch low
two hands
still clutch both shoulders
but not for long
my guttural ferocious "NO!"
shoots a vocal arrow
I turn, ready to strike

before me
the man
whose two hands
had been clutching both my shoulders
begs
trembling
"don't hurt me"
"please don't hurt me"
yes, now he is
begging
then skulks away
into the dark

the bus arrives
I climb the metal stairs
I go to work
later they tell me
six women were raped
at that bus stop
six women
obeyed
the two hands
clutching both shoulders
from behind

it is then the tears fall
for the six women
their pain
the continued trauma
but also for him

the way he shook in terror
trembling in the prison
of the abuse
once done to him
knowing only
to hurt or be hurt

imprinted indelibly
in the soul
we all share
my tears
then and now
open a portal
where we are
unmistakably one

decades later
I would hold your
two hands
I would not hide
I am still
prepared to fight
I will not sacrifice
my wholeness
still it is my deeply held wish
that somehow
you will be held
that somehow
you will be healed

so today
with my two hands
I create a wondrous bird of light
filled with my intention
that love find you
and hold you
long enough
to set you free

and I watch
that shining bird
take flight

I am Fine

I am fine
I am joyous as a wave leaping up onto the shore
I am fine
joyous as a wave

still every time I turn around
I see a face that isn't there
every time I turn around I see you

I am fine
I am joyous as a bird soaring high into the sky
I am fine
joyous as a bird

still every time I close my eyes
I feel you here right by my side
every time I close my eyes I feel you

I am fine
I am joyous as the sun shining down upon the earth
I am fine
joyous as the sun

still every time I go to sleep
I hold you deep inside my heart
every time I go to sleep I hold you

I am fine
I am fine

Kristen Guerrero

These days, when I am not working on an architectural deadline, or hosting creative arts / energy healing workshops, I am writing poetry. I have always loved the magic of words and appreciated the sacred resonance of poems.

My poems are largely inspired by the nature of my native upstate NY where I live with my husband and two children, and by the spiritual lessons I have received over the years from my teachers. Thanks to all of them, especially to Euric, Kieren, Katie, Master Isha, Master Derek O'Neill and Sri Satya Sai Baba.

I am so honored to have been a part of this supportive and beautiful poetry collective. I found this group of inspired poets through synchronicities I will never be able to explain. I allowed myself to become a poet, through Poetry Chapel, and I am grateful to this group, and to Chelan Harkin and David Tensen for their encouragement. To have my voice imprinted on these pages with the beautiful chorus of this collective is an amazing dream realized.

You can find more of my poems on most social media platforms @ Kristen Guerrero Poetry.

Ginkgo Tree

I asked the ginkgo tree for its wisdom,
hoping to learn
to synthesize the light in my veins
into nourishment,
for those souls,
(including my own),
who longed for God.

She answered,
"My love, I cannot teach what you already know.
We are both bridges between earth and sky,
rooted to this star,
reflecting what light we can reach,
to help those souls,
(including my own),
see their way out of the darkness.

Drought

Walking in the grass
was a violence of
crackling and breaking,

I sat poked and needled,
in solidarity with
the blades made brittle by absence.

It didn't seem possible
the field was ever green,
or if it would ever remember
the supple softness of love,
after the length of lack.

My gratitude for
the graying sky,
intensified with
the strengthening wind,
as mercy began to baptize the earth.

I asked the downpour
to soak my soul,
and I implored the grass
to teach me how to be restored,
how to allow transformation,
in the flood of love.

Little Drummer Girl

At 5 years old
you were moved
to perform a music show.

You gathered
your red plastic drum
and your family together.

Lending solidity
from the hearth
of our old stone fireplace,

you tried to
sing and drum
away the heaviness,

bright yellow drumsticks
thunking
on the plastic.

Only the
laughter
crescendoed,

dull drum beating
breaking
your heart,

as expressing
love
felt like shame.

I can whisper
to you now:

"You chose
so bravely
to heal this,

to beat against
the vibration
of dysfunction.

Your song
is a gift
they cannot open,

your little voice
not loud enough
to wake them.

But you tried,
love.

Keep drumming
little one."

Starlings

If I can see
the changing
flight patterns of many birds
are set in motion by one,

If I can feel
the shift as
one subtle intention
manifests across the flock,

If I can know
it is possible
for a singular expression
to spill itself in patterns
across the cosmos,

Then-

If I can manage
to lift my head up
towards the sky
and choose happiness,

the whole world
might also smile
together in the sun.

Dream of Teacher

Busyness had made me late,
running through darkness,
when the street opened to reveal him,
haloed,
golden,
under the light post,

"Hey," I called,
"Is the dance lesson over yet?"

Smiling arms,
a rush of homecoming,
the hearth of his heart,
bhakti tears in lovelit eyes,
belonged,
unforgotten,
in ancient rosy incense air,

Teacher
had waited for me.

Overjoyed,
I remembered dancing together
soul light blazing,
love-soaked,
cocooned in stars,
one in being,
across lifetimes without end.

Susie Rafferty Glad

Poetry writing is a natural way for me to release big feelings. A heart-on-sleeve empath, intuitive, and word catcher, my poems often emerge randomly, drawing inspiration from unwitting beings.

I credit my Mom (spelling bee coach), and the nuns, for my aptitude turned fervor for the written word. Many a procrastinated term paper was accomplished swiftly, at the memory of angry nuns rapping on my knuckles. Born and raised in Pittsburgh, PA, I am the youngest of five offspring raised by devout Irish Catholic parents. My wise, unassuming folks modeled finding the magic, humor, and beauty in all.

A dreamer and lover of people––I seek truth, equity, authenticity and self/other understanding. As a career psychotherapist, one driving passion of mine is empowering the underdogs of the world to shine. Next I envision casting different reflections into the light via songwriting, painting, and comedy.

My sweet husband Tom and I, and our kitty Holly, divide our time between our sea house in Mendocino and the North Bay in CA. We share three delightful adult children, all relocated to the East Coast.

I am thrilled to publish my poetry for the first time, alongside this brilliant array of fellow writers.

Find me on Facebook or email me:
littledeercreekangel@yahoo.com.

Until

None of us know when our church bells will ring
and when the bagpipes will sing us home

I lounge on the deck this lazy Sunday morning
as if I have all the time in the world
gazing at our deer family in the ivy
pondering how they feel inside
wondering what they think

Do they believe they are immortal too
they preen each other
nibble on abundant greens
the trickling fountain invites them to a drink
do they miss their lost loved ones
and imagine this may be their fate soon

I muse on the deer and mourn my loving Mom
who died two years ago today
after hanging on desperately for her own dear life

That afternoon before those sad dark hours
she grabbed my bra straps as if to embrace me
but instead her tender arms begged
her eyes pierced my eyes
her cracked voice pleaded:
"Come on, come on, let's go, let's go, let's GO"

God only knows exactly where
but I imagine
she wanted to visit her garden just below
yet cruelly too far for her to see or smell
flowers she masterfully grew and tended to so well

A few months prior when I hopped off the plane
Mom whispered, "maybe YOU can save me"
I tried Mom, I tried, I did not want to let you go

I recall she and sister and I out shopping for trees:
"You girls think I am going to live forever,
I'll be 6 feet under when that tree is 6 feet tall!"
Mom's wit was equal to her practicality
ultimately under no pretense about her mortality

My deer friends bolt and interrupt my reverie
reminding me of their fragility
I want them to be free from strife
precious mortal beings not unlike my dying Mom
I vow now to always honor this tender life

Until the church bells ring
Until the choir ladies sing
Until we have our proper burials
Until the bagpipes sing us home

Summer in the City

the Uber drivers lift me up
giving me a sense of belonging and care
dutifully they take me to my heart's desire
some friendly, some silent, looking stoic
some glancing in their rear-view mirror

some rock their gospel, pop, hip hop, or jazz
frazzled, bedazzled, laughing their socks off
some avoiding my loving stare

yet some stop me hard in my tracks
utterly disarming, charming, fascinating
deep beyond words that ten minutes can bring
a captive audience to our play
sadly my ticket only takes me to the opening scene
mystery awaits in those wings

transformed into a curious child
fixated on my mysterious new friend
accepting the heart invitation
entering into each other's worlds
knowing some forces are determined to divide us
I see you in me, will I see you again?

my hand grazes the door handle, lingering
anticipating
one last abiding gem

Raw

Weep your rawness away
bleed into the edges of your soul
away from the peering glances of the bystanders
away from the hushing epiphanies of the judges
away from the ones who think they know
away from the spiritual bypassers
away from the ones who fear the depth
away from the sting of the bow

Born alone
we die alone
your heart is your own
dive now
into that sweet spot of your deepest naked truth
revealing the raw tenderness of youth
where once you labored to hide those tears

Dive now to deeper waters
dive now, my friend
dive deep once again
below
you remember how
let go
there is an oyster there
your pearl awaits
within

The Light

Just beyond that door
just behind those trees
gazing at an ocean of possibilities
waiting patiently for me

Just beyond that door
just behind those trees
yes, I hear an invitation
to a journey of my own creation
it is whispering to me

Just beyond that door
just behind those trees
now the sea is shouting
come play with me

Just beyond that door
just behind those trees
here comes my friend the light
she's beckoning me, relentlessly
We dance into the night

Just beyond my door
just behind my trees

Invisible Woman

the white hair defines her
absolved and resolved
stands comfortably alone
walks into a room
feels the tone
it's her time

the invisible woman
they shrink her in size
the glances go past her
without compromise

the invisible woman
rankles powers that be
under the radar
where no one can see

the invisible woman
superpower times ten
poses no apparent threat
just a woman and her pen
as candid words fly off the page
rousing sleepers
from their rest

Michael Harrison

I grew up in Melbourne, Australia, a city where the seasons flow gently ... and often! In Melbourne the idea that 'if you don't like the weather right now, just wait five minutes' is amusingly apropos.

I have written all my life as a way of making sense of myself, my relationships and my world. Words have been an important and dear companion on my journey. It is only in recent times that I have thought about a tentative sharing of some of these words.

I am an educator ... and I thank the universe for the privilege of being so. To work with the young, and those who work to educate the young, is to see the future created before our very eyes.

I am also a person of faith. You may well glean from my writings that it is a Catholic version of faith that inspires and frustrates me in equal measure ... but from many conversations I have had with others of different faiths, this seems to be a universal experience of believing in any communal way.

It would be wonderful to hear your thoughts on anything you find here ... and it would be consoling to know that somehow, somewhere out there in our shared world's vastness, these thoughts are finding other hearts and lives.

I can be contacted at harrymick60@gmail.com.

Thank you for visiting these poems!

Sad Arse Hope

you don't want
sad arse hope

the hope that things will get better
while citing the
travails of the
world

the hope that all will be well
while battening the hatches and
letting down the
steam

the hope that somewhere
sometime light will shine again
while blowing out the candles to
save the
wax

you don't want sad arse hope
putting out the rubbish and
turning off the
light

hope has to lean in

hope has to sight the horizon and
walk the charted
path

knowing
of course knowing
that when you get there another
horizon will be summoning
and then another

but that's the hope

that despite the
shrugged shoulders the
scorning word the
pitying look the
contempt

there is life in the walking

in the carrying souls along by
the depth of your resolve and
the breadth of your
conviction

in the light it lends
to the path

in the hope

I Alone

I alone can climb the mountain
Sail the seas, forge the streams
I alone can thwart the demons
Of our disconcerting dreams

I alone can buoy the broken
Bind the wounds, seek the lost
I alone can build the bridges
For the rapids to be crossed

I alone can rail for justice
Tell the truth, do what's fair
I alone can raise the standard
For the world's beleaguered prayer

I alone can ask the question
Smite the door, turn the key
I alone can heed the summons
To the grace God gifted me

And when the time has come to ending
To account for all that occurred
I alone can stand in the brightness
Of the searing implacable Word

The Earth to Hold You

When words fade before the sun has even set
and touch lingers
in that twilight time

when the memory of joy is forsaken for wish
and a whisper of truth
no longer settles the dusk

when the tears of doubt have lost their sting
and the heart's questions
harden and bake

when honesty denies its own reward
and pain lingers distantly
in a past sigh

then is the time to brace
for the falling

then is the time to let the earth on which you lie
hold you in its
gentle insistent hope

Good Friday Leaders

Did the authorities come to watch that day
The leaders who played their part
The powerful with much to lose or gain
The mercenaries bigots and upstarts

Did they line the streets for the parade
Watching insults rain down as spittle
Or with job well done did they skulk away
As he was surrounded and belittled

Did they cheer on the savage beating
That men can bestow on men
When that ancient simmering brutality
Is given licence to reap again

Did they see the women who loved him so
Drowning in their sea of loss
Could they picture their own frantic mothers
Following such an accursed cross

Did they join the chorus of the fevered cast
Smug at the plans they had sworn
Or did a sliver of guilt deep in their soul
Leave their derision hollow and stillborn

And at its end did they bother to meet
At the place where wood met bone
Where the cross was raised for all to see
A Christ broken and alone

More likely it is they washed their hands
As Pilate is said to have done
And hurried home for breakfast
Before the beating had even begun

For those with much to lose or gain
Are forever complicit in the lie
That the dangerous truth of one man's life
Can ever be sentenced to die.

Venka Payne

I live in the Columbia River Gorge, in the Pacific Northwest of the United States. I take inspiration from the fragments of Ancient Forests that still exist here. Writing and painting have always been intertwined in my process, but it was painting that I first identified as my mode of expression and considered to be "my work". Recently I've been writing more poetry, which flows from my process when I paint, and from simply wanting to express things in words.

Each of my three poems for this collective I wrote during the time I attended Poetry Chapel led by Chelan Harkin. This was my first experience sharing my poetry with other people, and I found it inspiring and validating. It opened me up in a way I hadn't expected. A deep bow to Chelan, and David Tensen, for hosting this sacred space. Each poem is dedicated to someone who has inspired me or come through in the poem in some way.

My purpose in this life is to convey my love for Ancient Forests and bring that love into people's homes and lives. This is a constant theme for both my writing and art. Please receive my gratitude for connecting with my work in this way. You can also connect with me online, on Facebook or on my website www.woeldart.com.

"The word for world is Forest"
~Ursula K Le Guin

Permission

For Andrew Pate

I gave myself permission
one day
to write

instead of
doing things
or even
painting things

and now
I need less
and less
consent

to put down
words on paper.

Was that so hard

saying yes
to black marks
on a white sheet

permissing
the silent impulses
of my mind

They'd have just as soon
stayed that way

a wisp of wind
in the Ancient Trees

But somehow
they emerged

Some one
saw some thing
in some one's head

If you bring forth
what is within you

Words beget Words

It said.

"If you bring forth what is within you, what you bring forth will
save you. If you do not bring forth what is within you, what you
do not bring forth will destroy you."
~Jesus, The Gospel of Thomas

Sturgeon Moon

for George Dawson, 1935-2018

Part I

What pulls you
from the muddy depths

Oh bottom feeder
fathomless ancient creature
spiny forgotten wonder

Were you in that other world
ugly or beautiful
and what are you now

Who was or is
the oldest the biggest the strongest
the wisest of you

What would you have me know
under the still waters
of this pale moon night

You who abide the depths.

Part II

I could have been in the Forest tonight
among the Silent Trees

I traded a moonlit swath of Old Growth
for an expanse of emptiness

shadows for light
water for breath.

Show yourself!

Just for a moment

Don't even think just race to the surface
shedding glints of silver as you go.

Pierce the air
Emerge
as if you've never breathed before.

Look! We share this moment
suspended in illumination

Is this the glimpse
of truth I sought

Is it

Shall I follow you down
to the depths whence you came.

Buffing the Wax

for Clemens Starck

Of all the things
I could be doing
on this hundred and two
end of July day

here I kneel
out in the shop
nose an inch from the surface
of a painting on panel
soft sheepskin rag in hand
upper arm and shoulder aflame

buffing the wax

vertical rubs, I've found, are best,
easiest, make it possible
to get the leverage that's needed
to get that sheen

Slowly, and not without some pain
the shine begins to appear
in streaks across the paper

It's slow going

I turn my head
to catch the correct angle of light
to reveal the shine.

A vast expanse of dull, unpolished surface
appears at eye level
a green horizon stretching
to the edge of the Earth.

My arm goes limp.
What is the point of this?
I implore aloud

The spiders in their dark corners don't answer.

I could have just varnished and been done.
And how do I know when it's done?

Familiar questions, I muse.

But more interesting...
Why is wax so enticing...
The waxiness of wax

Time to turn up the tunes
invoke the heroes
alive and dead
and keep on working

buffing the wax.

Note from the editor.

During one of the Poetry Chapel gatherings, Venka's young son burst onto the Zoom camera announcing he was also writing poetry. We asked if he'd share something he'd been writing with his mum in their special poetry book. He read this gorgeous little piece and I felt it just had to be included in this collection.

Leo, you can now say you are a published poet!

You are loved!
David Tensen

Catching Lizards

by Leo Savarese

Little lizard
so still and sweet
you run so fast
on little lizard feet

I want to catch you
if I can
and hold you gently
in my hand.

Charlotte Robertson

I grew up in Toronto as a free spirited child. My mum 'Wacky' and my dad 'Hughie' were artistic and social. Their creativity and commitment to family were foundational for me. Their friends were diverse and exciting.

In my sixth year, I was crouching in the sunlight and sniffing a flower; the essence of the moment transported me, and has remained a touchstone in my life. A powerful voice in my head insisted that I never forget this epiphany and that my task in life was to be aware of and to release any conditioning of my mind.

In my twenties I experienced a sustained descent into the dark night of the soul. My yearning to ease my nightmares led me to an extraordinary woman. Marion Woodman, a Jungian analyst, showed me how to mine my interior landscape and use the archetypes in dreams to heal myself, to deepen my awareness of life. Accordingly, I remain acutely aware of my dream world: the images inform much of my poetry.

My work experience as a professional photographer, an international trade specialist, homeopath and a hypnotherapist have helped to keep me grounded in the world of form. Each time another epiphany arose I'd write it down. My late friend Carol saw my little pieces as poems to share. Chelan and David have introduced me to the craft of poetry, and all its challenges, for which I am grateful.

Little Bird

i was a bird

not just any bird

but a tiny
plain
brown
bird

in ecstasy

in my beak
i carried
a fine
thread
that glittered
in the sunlight

i was
hopping
and flying
from
branch to branch

weaving
a sari
for my
Beloved

The Banquet

I was seated
on the earthen floor
at the back
of the banquet hall
with many others

Gabriel came up to me
and beckoned me to follow

and we wove our way
to the front
where Jesus was dining
with his disciples

looking into my eyes
the Prophet said
"Charlotte, the trouble with you is
you want to bring
all your friends
on this journey"

my heart leapt
with joy at the thought
and I smiled

"I know"

Marion

be like the wind
darling
as the world
shakes through
its agonies of
sorrow and despair

allow your body
its softness
and its strength
as rain
drops
from your eyes

with your cheeks
brush every element
in nature
and with your lips
kiss every creature

carry the messages
of love and protection
from all the
prayer flag threads
encircling mountains
plains and oceans

be like the wind
darling
and let your
rising currents
uphold the birds
as they glide and soar
above this parched
and hungry earth

Vision Quest

I was alone
in Los Padres Forest

as my inner stories
settled with the dawn
this is what happened

in the
silence of waking
two owls
hooted
and
red tailed hawk
swept past

a mother doe
whinnied
and showed me
her fawn

gray fox came
a white dot
by his nose

both ears rose
and he darted

then I heard
the shots
of restless hunters
in the glen

later
fox returned

and
trembling with excitement
I felt
the warmth of fur
against my skin

together
in silence
we watched
the setting sun

Lisa Perskie Rodriguez

I like to think I was born and raised in two Americas as my life has been split between the two continents and my work profoundly influenced by both. I was born in New York City, brought up in New Jersey, and went to a private high school and college in the northeast. Marrying a Colombian man led me to a whole new world. I lived in Colombia for 21 years, where I had my son and daughter and launched my career in international education and school administration.

While there, I had the opportunity to serve the Wayuu community in the Guajira region. The friends I made inspired me with their wisdom of living close to nature and to God. They approach life as a spiritual journey. In my own journey, I have been guided by the teachings of the Baha'i Faith which continually inspire me in my path of learning, transformation and connection, and service in bonds of love with others.

After leaving Colombia, I worked for two years in Guatemala. In my last post before retirement I served for eighteen years as the Executive Director of School of the Nations in Brasilia, Brazil.

Now I'm blessed with four precious grandchildren and time to dive into a deep personal passion: writing! I am writing poems and working on the sequel to my debut fantasy novel: Laela and the Moonline.

For more information visit
www.lisa-perskie.com

How Do You Tend
The Garden of Your Heart?

Clear your heart
from brambling fear
and the hardness
of unyielding thoughts
opening the loamy
terrain for tender
shoots of hope
that will, yes, they will arise
into promising blossoms
and ever mighty trees
harboring your life

Gather seeds from
the gnarled-
wisdom laden trees
fruitful with the fragrance of love-
seeds worthy of endless generation
dedicated to godly veneration

Do you let your garden go?
or fancifully imagine it
with silver bells and cockle shells
and fairy tale wishes-
that do not grow?

Your soul garden is God's trust
for a life of abundance
a bestowal to you
and a source of renewal
to others
water it with kindness
and weed it from
snakes that snare its
roots and fruits

Tend all worthy seeds
in their yearning
to reach towards the sun
and flourish in beauty
and future strength

Celebrate every tiny curl
of feathery growth.

All begins and ends so humbly.

Nana and Gabe Poem

Crooked in my arm
I look over at your curly eyelashes
and plump hand holding the book with me
my youngest grandchild

Making me unmistakably
older and elderly
treasuring the fleeting years
in which you are too young
to worship youth

Still too young
to join the tribe
that seeks identities
without connection
in a world where family
can mean brand and logo

Still too young
to think of beauty
as the closest approximation
to airbrushed models
wrapped in consumer goods

My oldness has
excommunicated me
from prominence

from the tribes who claim
power and relevance
perchance, I am the meek
who will soon inherit the earth
in death at least

I am trying not to cling
to your innocence
just remember the moment
our shared meekness
in different phases of life

I ask you
which is your favorite room
in this graciously appointed home
where my visit
is a pilgrimage of love
and you think long and hard
and I am guessing
the playroom or the sunroom
and you say
'your' room
the visitors' room
where we are snuggled together
treasuring the moment
the gift we are to each other.

Enable and Ennoble Me

Dear God, please
enable and ennoble me
to see and know
divine reality
as the template
of my life
Its ocean my screen
Its infinite containment
Where I dive and surface
bathed in light.

Ennoble and enable me
to inscribe life-generating
words on the tablet
of my heart and
and see beyond
black-twig forms
scrolling
waves of ink
to possibilities
arising like birds
from the shores
lifting me

Into realms
reveling in meaning

Enable and ennoble me
to hear the hum
of the galaxies
emanating
from an ever
giving source
connecting all
in the anthem
of love
lifting souls
from dust into angels

Enable and ennoble me
to leave the prison
of self
to seek limitless closeness
beyond the world
beyond the words.

Laura E. Scheele

I am a poet, empath and a lifelong word nerd, disguised as a stay-at-home suburban mom in Indiana. I may be a late bloomer, but that's assuming there's a right and wrong time to blossom. When I was a child, my family worked for the military, so I've learned many zip codes. After ten years in Europe, we settled in Bloomington, IN. There, I went to high school, then college for elementary education at Indiana University. I taught for several years before deciding to stay home with my kids. I have three wild, amazing and humbling children. My husband, Robbie, is my greatest friend and encourager, the love of my life.

My poetry is composed of the stuff that made me. My mentors have been many: dead poets, teachers who saw my capacity to write before I had the audacity, trauma that taught my "too sensitive" soul to catch fire, and flowers, which bounce back after a long winter. Music and faith have been common influences sewn throughout the pieces of my life. Music brings me peace and the permission to feel emotions; writing brings me life and the ability to communicate those emotions. Faith, I found in the Catholic church, where I'm grateful to sing now. The love poured into my poems comes from an unconditional God and my ever-supportive family and friends. I am deeply thankful to Chelan and the many inspiring writers of this group.

I'd love to hear from you via Facebook or email:
lauraEpoetry@gmail.com

Of Mountains and Organs

as we gaze up at the mountains
you ask me
how it is a mountain's moved,
I say, "all this talk of moving mountains
I think we have our task confused"

immense oceans and grand canyons
skies and stars in their vast chorus
prove we're small, and merely here
to love what is before us

in the plaza of San Marco
there stands a bell above the clock
it rings five minutes till the hour
then once more, at the top

a sign an older generation
sets the stages for the new
the bricks were laid upon the wall
many years before the roof

oh, these mighty mountain movers
so quick to claim their mastery,
yet nameless souls carved flutes from stone
before thunderous organs sang in Greece

but, just like the intricate pipe organ
a tool for grace, it plays its part
we are not gods or giants
just simple strings of harps

and why would we want to move the mountains?
when the universe
lives in a single beating heart

Lake Maxine

There's a body of water near the Michigan border
one might misunderstand enough
to call a glorified pond
but for me, it was a kingdom
of freedom and minnows
and a collection of very old docks
unincumbered by the pressures of school
I spent summers with bare feet,
paddling every corner of that place
Maxine was always watching
smiling and rocking, sometimes smoking
on her rusty red porch
Bloody Mary in hand, she was a queen
breathing in the sparkling ripples
singing to the sunsets, as they turned
the whole lake pink
she didn't have much voice,
but a song for everything
In my younger days she was pontoon rides
and competitive euchre games, way past bedtimes
telling ornery kids to take a long walk
off a short dock
tube radios playing gritty gospel songs
I was older before I noticed
her lake was surrounded by trailers
older still before that meant anything
weightless on my row boat, I'd catch a painted turtle
and I was richer than a king
thank you, for that simple wisdom, Maxine

Super Human

it's magnificent that
as humans,
we have the unique capacity
to completely reinvent ourselves,
in the middle of our lives
imagine, for a moment,
a hippopotamus, in his big mouth glory, exclaiming,
"water is no longer my thing, I think I'll grow wings
and learn to fly, to live a weightless life!"
well, no, I don't believe that could be
but, by George, a trashman can
earn his pilot's license and
BOOM the trucks
are history

it's magnificent that
there are no rules in stone to claim
you must stay exactly who you are right now
even characters of the Bible changed their name
Julia Childs learned to cook at forty
Harry Potter was born from a midlife crisis
all this to say
your heart might always beat the same
birthmarks and genetics may hold their place
but you can live a life that's truer
the timid can be the teacher
the judge a humble servant
you can do this, because
you're human

One for Her

Mary, the day we met,
or I met you, was also the day you died.
It's a shame, but you have stayed every moment
present, in my ears and pens, all the words I write,
a tribute, of sort, to one who simply dared to ask
what I'd like my life to hold. Your silky thoughts
coiled around my heart   and mind, down my
famished fingers, then   seeped deep into my
bones. Mary, you painted   mysteries of this place
in bouquets of phrase upon a page. You had no fear
to write of truth, of God, of geese, or fruit. You were
grateful for the flowers, and I'm so thankful I found
you. Mary, my voice within had long been hushed, a
ghost left lingering in neural hallways, singing
sonnets of something more,

begging

to

be

heard.

Your seed gave prompt permission to my words.
How could I ever thank you, Mary Oliver?
What a joy it is to

write,

to

dream

to whisper songs unto the moon, and let the rain fill
old wounds. I hold this pencil with hungry hands,
stumble over   rhymes of roses,   but I know this
is my chance,   to prune   the gift   you planted

Lady Moon

somewhere a piano plays
a haunting evening serenade
the horizon's dressed in deepest blue
she enters
lovely lady moon
she rises up her stairs of stars
starts her nightly masquerade
her window waltz across the room

wistful blind romantics fall
for her mask of mere reflection
the flirtatious grinning golden girl
the foolish man's perception

there is more than meets the eye
a strength to ebb and flow the tides
a song to cause the wolves to sing
a light
from sun she's channeling
she exposes monsters of the dark
awakes the tightly sleeping hearts
she guides the lost and wandering

a heroine in glowing dress
the Lady Moon fades out of sight
she is not your glamorous mistress
but the untamable poet
of the night

Paul Senn

I grew up in Evanston, Illinois, a college town neighboring Chicago. The mix of Midwest US culture and the influx of college students and professors from all over the world mirrored my internal life.

My parents were also interesting contradictions—my professor father, the son of a Wisconsin home-builder, loved the forest, camping, and fishing as much as teaching economics. I myself became a mix, never quite comfortable in one groove: football, lacrosse, math and science by day; guitar and consciousness explorations by night. Sometimes a bike ride to the Bahai Temple in Wilmette for respite on weekends.

It was the late 60s and 70s and I was blessed to have a small circle of equally odd close friends. My nickname became "jock-freak". Really, the name still applies! After a career in high-tech, I changed my stripes to mental health counselor. I love the process of merging the two worlds.

My poetry reflects all of this (I hope). I have also written a screenplay I hope to have produced someday.

You can see more of my various musical, visual and written pursuits at thetau-gallery.com.

I love to communicate with readers.
Email me at psenn@thetau.io, or find me on
Facebook as PaulRSenn. Thanks for reading!

Death Bed Conversation

I should have loved you more deeply
  You loved me from where you stood
I should have spoken more clearly
  Your spirit spoke to me every day
I should have dreamed bigger
  I heard your soul dreaming

I should have spent less time wondering
what more I could have done
  That I can agree with

Is this what real talking and real listening is?
Why didn't we do it more?
  There you go again

Can I have just a few more days?
  I don't know. But I do know
  I can read this poem to the world for you
Maybe our voices will carry to a lot of people
  For a long time

Real talking
  Real listening
  Maybe rest now?
I can rest
now

Into Light

I dropped the search for serenity
Gave up watching
The words
As I typed
From this new place
Where nothing matters
I wrote the darkness
Into light

No Dogs Allowed

This is a serious poem
Because
After all
We BOTH know
Poetry is serious business
No Dogs Allowed!

I won't waste your time
Or try to drizzle drazzle you
With idle
Frizzle frazzle
I don't let just anybody in here
No Dogs Allowed

Yea, this one dog-eared
Black-eyed pea-brained
Schnauzer of a poem
Keeps coming around begging for rhymes
But I refuse to let him in
He has no class
And I know you are allergic

I only entertain the highest ideals here
You won't find any yipping yammering
Onomana-pana-poodles
Or graphic novella terriers
Or flirty newfys in heat.

No Dogs Allowed!
Shirt and Shoes Required!

Now that I am a serious poet
I tolerate these puppies
That keep wandering around the word hood
Sometimes I let them sit in the prologue
Or do tricks on Instagram

If they are really good
I translate them into French
And read them to people
Who don't know French

But I will not let them throw me off
My distinguished and well-honed style
I am after all
Now keeping the company of gods
I must be tolerant of the riff-raff
I was once one of them
I still contain in me
A terrified son of a sophisticated bitch collie
She hoped I would become so much more
And look!
Here I am
Finally
A Serious Poet

Best Wishes

I found a get well card among the flyers and false
promises
with only your initials as the return address
I will never write back
except in this journal
where I can let words flow as they will
When I first woke up, I heard them say
"His eyes are fluttering"
these strangers caring for a stranger
in the deep deep hospital night
The way they reached out to me
I reached out to you like that
in the middle of our last night
Trying to save our life
There is care in their distant voices
the nurses and the specialists
coming in like some lost radio wave
"You are in a hospital, you are going to be ok"
"Tell us 5 things you can see"

Probing eyes above masks, bathed in fluorescents,
my fragile body in pajama blue
"4 things you can hear"
the monitor, the heartbeat
the clatter of some metal tray, shuffling footsteps
the hissing air
Yes, I can taste, touch, smell
But I do not answer, my senses drift inwards

I am falling back
Into another bed, another room, another time
I feel the sensation of you washing back over me
My mind travels south and starts singing
A country song, written on the fly
5 ways I used to hold you
4 songs we used to sing
3 memories to bring me back to
what we could have been

The guardian angels
start singing a different song
In their stylish blue pajamas
Interrupting my descent
Into my country mourning
They call me back to this beeping humming room
their rhythmic reassuring tones are just right
I will be ok
Thanks
I just needed a reminder
This is not the first time I learned how to die
after all,
I've been shot through the heart before
And survived
Yes, well said
Best wishes
For my speedy
Recovery

Velusia Van Horssen

When the poetry spirit came for me some years ago, it seemed to put a tap root into some fertile mulch that had evolved naturally over decades of spiritual midwifery, and began growing its own garden.

Cherishing the connection, I've come to understand its preference for moonlight, and the ashes of my day, so we have made an exchange ... I try to give it what it seems to enjoy, and it allows me to gather its bouquets.

It is making an activist of me, walking me through doors I am surprised are in front of me and showing me how to 'stand for love' ... joining me in part of an intervention that has come for us all.

Dorothy Day proclaimed that 'the world will be healed by beauty', and attending the Poetry Chapel has led those of us sitting in its pews many steps closer to having a true voice in its chorus. Thank you.

I say that I am an essential and contemplative poet because of the 25 years of in depth essential work that led to the contemplative space I work from. If you would like to receive my poetry you are welcome to join me on Facebook. My email address is exchange@velusia.org.

A Prayer for This

Flower so beautiful, but let me be seed!
Never to lose the painful bliss
of breaking open, or the force
of the quickening within.

I don't know how one longs
for what one already has,
but I do...

Call it gratitude ... I only know that it
plunges most willingly back to itself.

Oh, let me linger here in this black perfection
and harvest the sparks that burn through or
land so lightly, on tip toe, fully formed.

Is this a lighthouse being built, or the sun itself!
It receives and gives forth
in the same endless gesture of love.

Yes

John Lennon once told the story of attending
an art exhibition of Yoko Ono's that would decide
their future together.

In a corner of a room there was a ladder
that one must climb to reach a card
that could then be opened...

When he had climbed the ladder
and opened the card, there was
only one word written there, and
that word was YES.

Isn't 'Yes' the word we climb mountains
to see on the horizon?

Isn't it written in sunlight and a smile and the way
the young heron flew by just so?

Isn't it spelled out in ancient script
in all languages?

Doesn't it have the same affect
on all of our hearts?

Yes.

Apostles of the Present

we're a quorum of aptitude
waiting for instructions, which means,
not waiting at all, but listening

we're apostles of the present
though we have not forgotten...
garners of 'this' double as prayer
for the future

we aren't rocks, but flowers
so yes, we can be crushed
but the fragrance released will
never be recaptured

our destruction in form is part of the plan
like poppies dropping seed to wind,
then succumbing, the fragrance will reach
countless more

so we must paint, tell our stories
and write our mystic poetry from all
the countries in which we stand.
we are beacons of the heart

and cannot do otherwise
we'll call, and those that hear will
immediately behold the place inside
themselves from where we write

it's a kind of miracle, this, because
you cannot 'hear' poetry without becoming poet
look to what is awake in you
nodding ... knowing

I am a woman harvesting wisdom from
centuries, but now ... through 'this'...
it's the same wisdom, set in water, blooming still
though in colors on a spectrum just revealed

because you are part of this quorum,
your eyes are key
though your ears
just the surface of hearing

like Beethoven we lost our attachment
to familiar sounds and began listening from
a depth of black velvet moved only by the moon

there we find the symphony
and even its name
and there we know our mother's womb
for the infinity it is

Sensing

here, take your socks off
and set your feet
in this cool watered stream,
feel the rounded stones
with the soul of your foot.

take the time it takes
for the water and the stones
to relay the message they hold
for your senses.

scan your body ... all of it.
tag those curious chambers of sensing
and perception ... even the alert and happy
one behind your pubic bone.

they all have the capacity to hear,
echo, and respond ... you need do nothing...
just feel your face forming expressions
that mirror the echo.

your eyes brighten and your beautiful
mouth becomes a perfect ‚O'
miraculously forming the entrance to
yet another chamber ... the one that
exchanges life with the source of it all.

After Machado

there are ways that we can
ask questions of ourselves
and each other
that set the beehive
in our hearts to work

in our willingness
to know what is
just beyond
that sense of loss
we carried

or to breathe life into
parts rejected
we'd be standing
true in our small
transparency clusters

letting the bees
do their work
of making white combs
and sweet honey
from our old failures

distilling pollen
from our very lives
seeing through new eyes
gathering honey

Elaine M Watson

I was born in Ilford, Essex, just outside East London in November 1953––a child of the 60s. It was the advent of the cultural revolution of sex, drugs and the Beatles. I went to a convent school that left me feeling like a fish out of water. The art room and literature lessons were my haven. I could get lost in painting, drawing and stories.

When I was 17, an introduction to the Sufi teacher and seer Mrs. Tweedie guided me to my husband whom I met at art college in 1975.

I have always written poetry, but never in the way it came to me during the Covid lockdown. It was as if a geyser in the desert sprang up and has been flowing ever since. Now I write at least three or four poems a week. Poems can come whole, or slowly. With some I have to grab paper and pen before they disappear; others are more measured. The Poetry Chapel has been a wonderful gift for me: sharing with other poets, and Chelan's influence has been exceptional. For me, God is an energy of unconditional love, my dearest wish is to transmit that through poetry.

A 12-step fellowship has helped considerably over the years with my addiction struggles.

I hold an honours degree in occupational therapy and have worked in mental health settings.

Please let me know if you enjoy my poetry.
Email me at ellymumbo@icloud.com or visit my
Facebook page Silent Source Poetry.

The Deer

The deer stood, like a blessing,
then vanished.
So still, so very still,
he stood.
I saw him; he saw me.

My still centre touched his,
and I am not the same anymore.
The moment here, then gone,
was like a lifetime of loving looks
that healed my heart in a nanosecond.

Now, I can live.
What happens to me
doesn't matter anymore.
I am on this human journey
'til I pass on to the next plane.

Here, You are waiting,
with the star-spun garment of light
that I will wear with joy, to dance madly
into eternity and beyond:
with You.

Mum

I inhale the scent of a rose,
and there I am with Mum,
back home in our front garden,
sixty-three years ago.
She's wearing a white dress
fifties style, cinched at the waist,
large blooms of pink roses
scattered on the skirt.

Her hair dark, short, wavy.
A natural grey streak at the front.
Bright blue twinkling eyes,
her head thrown back,
laughing.

Older now.
Her hair tinted a light blonde.
So careful she was to look good.
I remember seeing her in hospital
before she died, trying
to dab on her face powder.
'You've missed a bit, Mum.'
'I know,' she said,
'I haven't finished yet!'
She flashes her blue eyes at me.

Oh, how I still miss you.

Artifacts, Bones 'N Things

I contemplate the longevity
Of artifacts, bones 'n things,
Whilst flesh decays
In close-dark earth,
And only bones remain.

Buildings too,
Cup and saucer,
Diamond ring.
And Great Grandma's butter knife
Passed down
From hand to hand,
To butter
Who knows how many slices
For lives that
Finally gave up, like her
The flesh that bread sustained.

Things can feel no sadness,
Exuberance or joy,
They are simply there for us to use
And gainfully employ.
They go on and on and on

Whilst flesh dissolves
In close-dark earth
And only bones remain.

A cup cannot smell the coffee it holds
Or go and grind the bean.
Buildings cannot embrace you
Or ask you how you've been.
So giving up this body to ground,
Throwing off this body suit
Sets the spirit free
To go spinning and whirling
Dervish like
Throughout eternity.
Just bones remain
Down in the earth;
And finally we're free.

Earth Angel

*Awaken to the mystery of being here
and enter the quiet immensity
of your own presence.   J. O'Donohue*

For you have always been
and always will be.

When earth dries your bones
and you are no longer needed here
in bodily form,

the free essence of you
will continue somersaulting
and spinning through the cosmos

And all the other realms
that were beyond your limited
and grounded sight
will have access to your sacred presence.

They will sing choruses
to the joy of having you near.

It will not be an ego thing anymore.
It's just that you carried
earthly clothes for a while
until you were free to let them go—
Hallelujah!

Come Holy Spirit

Come Holy Spirit,
Show me that way
I do not know.

Sometimes,
It's like holding the straw
To stop me drowning.

And you are nowhere
To help.

Then, I turn, and see
That you can only appear
After many drownings.

And now I am learning
To breathe
Underwater.

Do you want to be part of a future
Poetry Chapel Book,
writing alongside best-selling
published poets?

You could be in the next collective;
writings, sharing, healing and learning through
poetry and publishing.

Limited spots per intake.

Visit www.poetrychapel.com
for more information.

SCAN WITH SMARTPHONE FOR URL
AND RELATED RESOURCES

Other Poetry Chapel Volumes
:
The Saving I Need
Poetry Chapel Volume 1.

2021

WINTERS NEVER LAST
Poetry Chapel Volume 2.

2022.

Also by David Tensen:

The Wrestle
Poems of divine disappointment and discovery.

2020

So I Wrote You A Poem
Poems of empathy on life, loss and faith.

2021

Support David by purchasing via
www.davidtensen.com

e: david@davidtensen.com

ig: @david_tensen
fb: /davidtensenwriter
tw: @davidtensen

Also by Chelan Harkin:

Susceptible to Light
Poetry by Chelan Harkin.
2020

Let Us Dance!
The Stumble And Whirl With The Beloved.
2021

Support Chelan by purchasing via
www.ChalanHarkin.com

e: chelanharkin@gmail.com

ig: @chelanharkin
fb: /Chelan Harkin Poetry

About the Editor & Publisher

Australian poet David Tensen brings form and beauty to our deep spiritual yearnings. Drawing from decades of experience in pastoral care, leadership and spiritual development, his poems have found their way into hearts of many. Raw, accessible, and prophetic, David's writings uncover pain and bring healing to it.

David is the founder of Poetry Chapel and fills his days helping authors across the world publish their own works.

www.davidtensen.com

David, his wife Natalie, and three children live in Queensland, Australia.

CPSIA information can be obtained
at www.ICGtesting.com
Printed in the USA
LVHW102328141222
735274LV00005B/520

9 780645 607208